SOMETIME LOFTY TOWERS
A Photographic Memorial of the World Trade Center

When I have seen by time's fell hand defaced
The rich proud cost of outworn buried age;
When sometime lofty towers I see down razed,
And brass eternal slave to mortal rage;
When I have seen the hungry ocean gain
Advantage on the kingdom of the shore,
And the firm soil win of the wat'ry main,
Increasing store with loss and loss with store;
When I have seen such interchange of state,
Or state itself confounded to decay,
Ruin hath taught me thus to ruminate:
That time will come and take my love away.
  This thought is as a death, which cannot choose
  But weep to have that which it fears to lose.

     William Shakespeare, *Sonnet 64*

DEDICATION

The Twin Towers stood long enough to let a majority of the people in them escape.
For this let us be profoundly thankful.

For all those who were obliterated in the collisions, trapped in the conflagrations, or overtaken by the collapses —
and the many thousands of their bereaved families and friends —
let us weep.

For a strength that will never collapse no matter how cruel the oppression,
let us look to our own collective will and spirit —
exemplified so poignantly by the heroic rescuers who died
striving in the name of mercy.

To them this work is respectfully dedicated.

SOMETIME LOFTY TOWERS
A Photographic Memorial of the World Trade Center

Introduction by
ROBERT HUTCHINSON

Remarks from
GOVERNOR GEORGE E. PATAKI

Photography by JAKE RAJS
and others

BROWNTROUT PUBLISHERS
San Francisco

Governor George E. Pataki's
Remarks to the Joint Session of the New York State Legislature
September 13, 2001

Today, we join together as a State, and as a Nation, to pray for the victims who were lost on one of the darkest days in American history.

We pray for the children who will go to bed this evening without their mothers and fathers. We pray for the mothers and fathers who've lost the children they loved. We pray for the husbands and wives who will return to empty homes. We pray for the firefighters, police officers and rescue workers who died while committing extraordinary acts of heroism.

We pray, also, for this great nation of ours, a nation that is free, a nation that is strong, a nation that is united in grief. For we know that the freedom we so cherish as Americans—for which hundreds of thousands of Americans have sacrificed their lives—exposes us to the wicked, the murderous, the cowardly forces of hate.

December 7th will always be known as a "Day of Infamy." So, too, September 11th, from henceforth, will be known as the day a dark cloud descended across America. But clouds always pass. The sun always breaks through. And we know as Americans that God's light will again shine across this land, and that our free and strong people will prevail.

The forces of evil that committed this atrocity have caused pain that will last for generations, pain that has claimed the lives of innocent men, women and children. But evil never prevails. Freedom, despite its vulnerabilities, will always prevail.

And I am confident that President Bush and a united American Congress will strike back—swiftly and strongly—against the forces of terror and the nations that harbor them. We will stand with the President in those actions.

New Yorkers have always stood strong, firm and together in times of crisis and human hardship. Already, we've seen the extraordinary heroism of our firefighters, police officers, rescue workers, and everyday citizens. We've seen the indomitable spirit of New Yorkers, pulling together to overcome the most horrendous, destructive and murderous act of terrorism in history.

We owe a deep debt of gratitude for the heroism of the thousands who have been risking and continue to risk their lives to help with the relief effort. We thank President Bush for the extraordinary aid he has provided. And we owe profound thanks to Mayor Giuliani and his team for the tremendous leadership they have shown.

This crisis has tested and will continue to test the resolve and the resilience of New Yorkers like never before. But ultimately, the courageous and resilient spirit of our people will prevail over this cowardly act of hatred.

Yesterday I was at Bellevue Hospital visiting injured firefighters. I stood at the bedside of a Lieutenant, thanked him for his courage, and told him he was a hero. And he smiled and said, in a thick New York accent: "What'd you expect? I'm a New Yorker." But then the smile left his face as he spoke about his partner, who was missing. With tears in his eyes, he told me his partner was the father of ten children.

I told him that those children will not be alone. We will stand with them. We will stand with all of these heroes, and we will stand with the children and family members they left behind. We will walk alongside them during this difficult time in their lives.

They are now a part of us. They will be a part of New York, and America, forever.

The people of this State are united as never before.

I've seen New Yorkers lined up for blocks, waiting to donate blood at Cabrini Hospital. I asked one woman why she was there and she said, "I have to be here." I've seen injured firefighters at St. Vincent's, begging to leave their hospital beds, so they could rejoin their comrades in the rescue effort. All across our State, people are volunteering to help however and wherever they can. In this time of crisis, we can draw strength from that spirit of unity, and from the compassion of our people.

There is nothing we cannot accomplish when we are united behind a common purpose. It is that common purpose that brings us here today. For today, the issues that occasionally divide us seem small. Today, we are united in our commitment to rebuild our great City and to rekindle the spirit of our people.

And because we are unified, I know we will be unanimous in the action we take today to help put this crisis behind us.

Make no mistake: We will not just survive this disaster. Nor will we simply overcome it. We, the people of New York, will join together, united in strength, and lift New York to its greatest day.

We face a long and difficult road. But we face it together.

These unspeakable acts have shattered our City and shocked our Nation. But they have not weakened the bonds that unite us as New Yorkers, and as Americans, as those who love freedom and, ultimately, as those who love one another.

Our strength will defeat this evil. Our spirit will overcome this atrocity. And, together, this land of the people, and by the people, will soar higher than even our beloved twin towers.

Thank you. God bless the great people of New York. And God bless America.

INTRODUCTION

Robert Hutchinson

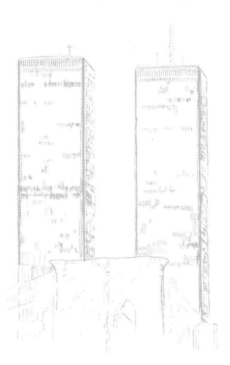

THE TWIN DIMENSIONS

On the eleventh morning of September, 2001, a global television audience witnessed in real time the unfolding of the most horrific terrorist mission in human history. Separated by fifteen minutes in order to ensure that the world's eyes were fastened on the second attack as it happened, two assassin airliners lumbered over Lower Manhattan and disgorged cataracts of exploding jet fuel into the colossal bodies of the Twin Towers of the World Trade Center, murdering with two fell strokes three thousand blameless souls.

The odor of death permeates every visual image preserved of that lovely fall morning's cataclysmic explosions and collapses. The humanity of the observer reels before the moral disproportion between the perceived offense and the actual punishment. For trying to make a living in a modern society deemed obnoxious by medieval clerics, thousands of workers deserve to die a horrible death?

Yet the images of that morning are scarcely less disorienting to the eye than they are to the conscience. The intellect of the observer reels at the physical disproportion between the disaster's causes and effects. The Twin Towers were so immense: each of them 1,360 feet high; 62 million cubic feet in volume; 750,000 tons in gross weight. Each of the attacking airliners was in comparison so small: 47 feet high; 20 thousand cubic feet in volume; 170 tons in weight.

Appropriate moral response in a free society depends on clear and careful understanding. Without in the least derogating the moral enormity and human horror of the World Trade Center disaster, we propose here to focus on its physical dimensions. Each Tower was thousands of times bigger than the object that brought it down. How was it physically possible? And how did the mechanism of destruction affect the survival rate of the office towers' occupants and rescuers?

THE TWIN TARGETS

In the assassins' crosshairs: the Twin Towers of the World Trade Center.

The germ of the idea for the World Trade Center sprouted in the 1950's in the brain of David Rockefeller. Touching his many levers of power, he effectively propagated his vision of a commercial and financial center of unprecedented magnitude and brilliance that would put beyond all dispute Lower Manhattan's claim to be the financial capital of the world.

Enthusiastically endorsed by other Wall Street tycoons and by political powerbrokers such as his brother Governor Nelson Rockefeller, the World Trade Center project swept away by eminent domain the gritty mix of small business and industry long established at the proposed site. In place of the traditional hodge-podge of buildings of assorted styles and uses, there grew two glistening monolithic office towers with the single function of accommodating an international plexus of financial and service corporations and state agencies. The World Trade Center Towers were commissioned to be not only the two tallest buildings in the world but also the first office complex ever to be threaded at construction with an integrated telecommunications network system.

In both the visible and invisible realms, then, the Twin Towers strove mightily to be regarded as icons of America's unparalleled economic power thrusting indomitably over the financial nerve center of the world. In this ambition, they conspicuously succeeded. On the morning of their destruction, the Twin Towers were the workplace of 50,000 employees of 700 firms from 28 countries renting over nine million square feet of office space.

The Towers were conceived by architect Minoru Yamasaki as identical twins of gigantic dimensions but minimalist geometry: each simply an elongated, slightly beveled orthogonal prism with a one-acre square cross section. The spatial relationship between the twins was very simple, too. Yamasaki just put two tall boxes side by side and then slid one of them southward. (On August 7th, 1974, it took French tightrope walker Philippe Petit forty-five minutes in a tricky wind to cross a cable stretched over the 131-foot-wide void between the tops of the Twin Towers.) So disposed, the eastern base of the North Tower and the northern base of the South Tower defined the western and southern edges respectively of the largest plaza in New York City, ostensibly patterned on Venice's celebrated Piazza San Marco.

The original white Italian marble cladding of the 5.3-acre, inward-sloping Austin J. Tobin Plaza had been replaced in 1999 by forty thousand radial blocks of brown and red granite, upon which were installed several monumental outdoor sculptures: including Fritz Koenig's bronze *Sphere* (1971), slowly rotating in the middle of the Olympic-sized Plaza Fountain. The Plaza's full name honored the potentate who oversaw much of the metropolitan region's massive public building boom from 1942 to 1972 in his capacity as executive director of the Port Authority of New York and New Jersey. The Port Authority is the quasi-autonomous public agency established in 1921 that owns the land upon which the WTC was built; that built and rented out the 12 million square feet of WTC office and shopping space (more than eight times that of the Empire State Building); and that had just completed in the summer of 2001 the conveyance of the last of its WTC holdings (the buildings 1, 2, 4, and 5 WTC and the subterranean shopping concourse) into private hands.

Ringing Tobin Plaza and sheltering it from the wind off the nearby Hudson River were six of the seven buildings, erected over the two decades between 1966 and 1987, that together constituted the World Trade Center. Until the morning of its destruction in 2001, the World Trade Center was the largest office complex in the world. On the Plaza's western edge stood the North Tower (properly, One World Trade Center): 110 stories; first occupied in 1970; construction completed in 1972; distinguished from its twin by its finial—a 358-foot-high transmission mast supporting ten main television antennas and topping out at 1,726 feet (which made 1 WTC on the morning of its destruction the tallest building in the world by one of the four official criteria for measuring building height: namely, height to antenna top). On the Plaza's southern edge stood the South Tower (2 WTC): 110 stories; first occupied in 1972; construction completed in 1973; distinguished from its twin by its topside observation decks from which as many as 80,000 tourists a day were afforded a 45-mile-radius panorama of America's biggest metropolis.

Off to the southwest, tucked between the Twin Towers, stood the Marriott WTC Hotel (3 WTC: 22 stories; completed in 1981). Around the Plaza's southeast corner was wrapped the Commodities Exchange Building (4 WTC: 9 stories; completed in 1977). Around the Plaza's northeast corner was wrapped the Dean Witter Building (5 WTC: 9 stories; completed in 1972). And off the Plaza's northwest corner stood the U.S. Customhouse (6 WTC: 8 stories; completed in 1975). Enclosing the 16-acre WTC superblock upon which these six buildings sat are four streets: West Street on the west (originally fronting the Hudson River), Liberty Street on the South, Church Street on the east, and Vesey Street on the north. Across Vesey Street from the Customhouse rose the 47-floor 7 WTC—last of the WTC buildings to be finished (1987) and the only one not on the Plaza.

Immediately beneath Tobin Plaza lay Manhattan's largest shopping concourse, called The Mall at the World Trade Center (until being renamed the Westfield Shoppingtown WTC when it was acquired by a Los Angeles REIT just two months prior to its destruction). This underground mall also served as the main interior circulation level of the WTC complex, traversed by 200,000 pedestrians every workday.

Each of the eight vertical faces of the Twin Towers themselves was a sheer wall of metal and glass 208 feet wide by 110 stories high—uniformly striated by 61 smoothly ascending silver-colored aluminum alloy-sheathed piers each 18¾ inches wide, framing 5,450 unusually narrow windows, each 22 inches wide. Seventy percent of the area of the Towers' facades was metal; only thirty percent was glass. A customized window-washing machine was able to judder up and down the facade at half-a-mile per hour, cleaning all the windows in a single 22-inch-wide stripe in just half-an-hour.

So vast and regular were the slender-serried facades of the Twin Towers that the observer's eye, sweeping round like Koenig's aqueous sphere from the meaner buildings in the east to the toplofty marvels on the west, was susceptible to rippling moiré effects as though of titanic sheets of watered silk. Asked at the press conference in January 1964 where he unveiled his final architectural plans for the Twin Towers why he hadn't designed instead just one tower 220 stories high, Yamasaki parried: "Hey, I didn't want to lose the human scale."

The North Tower boasted a structural height of 1,368 feet: making it on the day of its completion in 1972 the tallest building in the world; and on the morning of its destruction the fifth tallest building in the world (by the most commonly received criterion of structural height). Only negligibly shorter at 1,362 feet, the South Tower (2 WTC) briefly attained the rank of second tallest building in the world when it was completed in 1973, relegating the Empire State Building to third place; until all three were displaced down a notch by Chicago's Sears Tower just a month later.

In addition to its height above ground, each Tower subsumed six basement floors sunk 70 feet deep into porous glacial sediment so that its foundations could be keyed into the schist bedrock of Lower Manhattan. Also accommodated in the subsurface of the Towers was a converging tangle of tunnels for six New York City subway lines plus the PATH trains shuttling under the Hudson from New Jersey, all with WTC stations feeding into the underground concourse. The 10.8 million cubic feet of spoil from the excavations in the WTC compound of its 12-acre foundation—sealed against the incursion of groundwater under pressure from the Hudson River by a 3-foot-thick concrete "bathtub" retaining wall surrounding the basements of 1, 2, 3, and 6 WTC—were not wasted. They supplied the 23.5 acres of Hudson River landfill upon which was built the World Financial Center (the northern component of Battery Park City), which was linked to the WTC by a pedestrian bridge over the West Side Highway. Counting its basement, then, the gross volume of each Tower was 62 million cubic feet.

The weight of the structural steel lattice upholding each Tower was 100,000 tons. The corresponding 100,000 pieces of structural steel, all manufactured in the Midwest and West Coast of the United States, were hoisted into place high over the congested city streets by eight "kangaroo" cranes built in Australia for the purpose of "hopping" up each Tower's steel frame as it rose.

This great mass of steel was concentrated in two load-bearing tubes, one placed inside the other in a configuration pioneered by Yamasaki in his Seattle IBM Building (1964). The outer tube of each WTC Tower consisted of a square palisade of 244 cantilevered columns of hollow-box steel regularly spaced on 39-inch centers. All these external columns issued in packets of three from the spandrels of an 80-foot-high quasi-Gothic lancet arcade that defined the perimeter of the base of each tower and the height of its entrance lobby; thence the columns sprang upward the full height of the building. The function of this bristling steel exoskeleton was not only to bear the greater part of the compressive load of the building's weight but also to brace it against all overturning and twisting forces, in particular those imparted by wind pressures.

In a strong wind, the lateral resilience of the outer tube allowed a WTC Tower to sway as much as three feet from true perpendicular at the top. It was the densely distributed load-bearing capability of the outer wall, however, that saved 1 WTC from collapse after the chillingly premonitory terrorist attack of February 26th, 1993. A 1,200-pound nitrourea truck bomb exploded in the basement garage next to a support column under the south wall of the North Tower. The terrorists' frustrated intention on that day had been to cause the North Tower to topple southeastward into the South Tower, killing scores of thousands of office workers. The failure of the grand design of murder was no consolation to the six people who did die in the explosion.

The inner tube of each Tower, measuring 79 feet by 139 feet and consisting of a dense core of reinforced steel columns embedded in poured concrete, bore the balance of the building's load and also housed each tower's 102 elevators, four stairwells, and core components of the various mechanical systems (air, water, electrical, telecommunications). The inner and outer tubes were coupled at each floor by prefabricated steel trusses measuring less than 3 feet in depth but spanning the full 60-foot gap separating the outer and core tubes. Each of these horizontal truss systems distributed the superjacent weight of its 3-inch-thick concrete floor (such that each floor had a structural weight, including concrete pad and metal deck, of 2400 tons) to the two load-bearing tubes and also acted as diaphragms to stiffen the outer tube against lateral twisting and buckling stresses under wind-load.

Because the outer tube of steel columns was designed to be a highly redundant wind brace sufficient for the entire building—unlike conventional curtain-wall structures, which transfer lateral stresses into a building's interior via its floor membranes—the WTC Towers did not need any reinforcement by intermediate columns or load-bearing walls in the wide space between the outer and inner tubes. Moreover, an innovative three-tiered elevator system was designed by Otis Elevators to halve the number of elevator shafts normally required. Twenty-three high-speed express elevators communicated with "skylobbies" at the forty-first and seventy-eighth floors, at levels adumbrated on the exterior of the buildings by faint horizontal bands. From there, four banks of local elevators shunted traffic within each zone. Thanks to the spatial economies of the column-support and elevator systems, the WTC Towers afforded their tenants big unen-cumbered office spaces, featuring 75 percent potential occupancy of total floor area (half as much again as usual in office high-rises).

The total weight of concrete in each Tower, employed primarily in floor pads and core reinforcement, was 415,000 tons. Combining this figure with the weight of structural steel, the structural weight of each Tower surpassed a half-million tons. Fully clad, wired, equipped, furbished, and occupied (the Towers were 98 percent occupied at the time of their destruction), the operating weight of each Tower was increased by half as much again, to about 750,000 tons.

THE TWIN MISSILES

The assassins' weapons: two Boeing 767-200ER's (wide-bodied, low-wing, extended-range airliners with twin, podded turbofans underwing and two-class seating accommodation for 215 passengers), both departing Boston Logan International Airport minutes apart for non-stop flights to Los Angeles International Airport.

The first missile to strike was American Airlines Flight 11. It departed Logan at 7:59 am, scheduled to arrive in Los Angeles at 1:47 pm. There were 92 souls aboard: 81 passengers (including a cadre of five young male jihadist hijackers), nine flight attendants and two pilots. About fifteen minutes into flight, over Gardner, Massachusetts (60 miles northwest of Boston), the hijackers gained control of the cockpit. At 8:28 am, about 30 minutes into flight, over Amsterdam, New York (17 miles southwest of Albany), Flight 11 turned abruptly south, accelerated from cruising speed, then slowed to cruising speed again as it followed the Hudson River down to Manhattan. It covered 120 miles in 20 minutes, for an average post-turn cruising speed of 360 mph. At 8:48 am, Flight 11 slammed at cruising speed into the 94th-99th floors of the north face of 1 WTC. At 10:28 am, the North Tower collapsed all at once.

The second missile to strike was United Airlines Flight 175. It left its gate at Logan at 7:58 am and lifted off the ground at 8:14 am, scheduled to arrive in Los Angeles at 1:48 pm. There were 65 souls aboard: 56 passengers (including a cadre of five young male jihadist hijackers), seven flight attendants and two pilots. About 16 minutes into flight, over northwestern Connecticut, the hijackers gained control of the cockpit. Flight 175 veered off course in a southwesterly direction; narrowly missed colliding with American Flight 11 over Newburgh, New York (55 miles north of New York City); and then, over northeastern New Jersey, turned southeast to central New Jersey. Upon reaching a point 90 miles southeast of New York City at 8:45 am, United Flight 175 turned northeast at about the same time that American Flight 11 hit the North Tower. Having covered the last leg at an average cruising speed of 300 mph, Flight 175 struck the 78th-84th floors of the southeast corner of the South Tower at 9:03 am. At 9:59 am, the South Tower collapsed all at once.

Each Boeing 767-200ER had the following dimensions: wing span, 156 ft 1 in; fuselage length, 155 ft 0 in; overall height, 47 ft 0 in; maximum fuselage width, 16 ft 6 in. The volume of a Boeing 767-200ER is 19,529 cubic feet.

Without fuel, a Boeing 767-200ER weighs 126 tons. The standard Boeing 767-200ER has fuel capacity in its wings and central tanks for 69 tons, corresponding to a design range of 7,825 miles. Since the flight plans of Flights 11 and 175 involved less than half the design range, a prudent safety margin dictated a take-off fuel load of about 35 tons. Given that fuel consumption at the standard cruising speed of Mach 0.8 is about 5 tons per hour, the fuel-load of each

Boeing 767-200ER at time of collision probably exceeded 30 tons. Adding in cargo, the total weight of each Boeing 767-200ER at impact was in the vicinity of 170 tons.

Therefore, one WTC Tower (62 million cu ft) had the volume of 3,175 Boeing 767-200ER's (each 19,529 cu ft). Each WTC Tower (750,000 tons) weighed some 4,400 times more than the Boeing 767-200ER that hit it. This weight ratio between one WTC Tower and one Boeing 767-200ER equals that between a 275 lb human being and a 1 oz sparrow. But surely no common sparrow butting heads with a nose tackle—even if the former were flying at Mach 0.5—could make the latter crumble to dust. How could one Boeing 767-200ER of the same relative mass have such a devastating effect on a WTC Tower?

THE TWIN COLLAPSES

In seeking to account for how one airplane could have exerted enough force to bring down a building thousands of times bigger than itself, observers will naturally have recourse to the airplane's speed. It may well be imagined that a 170-ton hunk of metal hurtling through the air at 300 mph would pack a not inconsiderable force. Considerable enough to do a great deal of damage, certainly. But to knock down a whole Trade Tower?

No. The kinetic energy of each Boeing 767-200ER at the moment of its impact against its target tower was equivalent to that released by the explosion of one-third of a ton of TNT. The kinetic energy released by the collapse of one Tower was equivalent to that released by the explosion of 300 tons of TNT: almost a thousand times greater than that of the precipitating event.

The terrorist strikes did not succeed by application of overwhelming force, but by virtue of jujitsu sleight. By destabilizing just a few cards, the suicidal assassins were able to trigger the posthumous collapse of the whole house of cards under its own gravitational momentum. The crash of the Mach 0.5 Boeing 767-200ER was not in itself fatally destabilizing. The holes that the planes punched in the faces of the Towers cut only a fraction of the 244 steel columns in each outer wall. The very high redundancy of the load-bearing capacity of the outer wall meant that all the remaining columns were more than adequate to support the weight of the floors above the damage. What each crash achieved was the puncturing of the skins of the target and the missile, so that the jet fuel inside the latter could be injected like poison into the former. It was not the superficial trauma of the injection that killed the victim. It was the high body temperature induced by the incendiary poison.

There is very little physical difference between commercial kerosene and the Jet A turbine fuel that was released as liquid and vapor into the upper floors of the WTC Towers. Compared to commercial kerosene, jet fuel is somewhat heavier in order to give it a higher flash point, lower freezing point, lower vapor pressure, and lower volatility. Because jet fuel vapors are heavier than air, they can quickly spread long distances to ignition sources and then flash back. Mixed with air and exposed to an ignition source, jet fuel vapors will burn in the open and explode in confined spaces.

The hijackers in both Boeing 767-200ER's enhanced the release and dispersion of jet fuel within the Towers by smashing into them at about 27-degree bank angles. The airplane wreckage then plowed about halfway to the cores of the towers. Jet fuel burns at 1,830 degrees Fahrenheit. Although steel does not melt until it reaches a temperature of 2,606 degrees F, it loses half of its structural strength between 930 and 1,100 degrees F. Above 1,600 degrees F, the cold-worked microstructure of steel recrystallizes to a new set of more perfect grains, giving complete softening.

The WTC fire protection system—coats of chemical fireproofing for the steel and water sprinklers—was designed to withstand three to four hours of moderate-temperature internal office fires fueled by burning paper, furniture and walls. The initial jet-fuel fireballs, however, blew the insulation off the steel of the affected floors and disabled the sprinkler systems. Then, over the next hour or so, the burning of jet fuel and office combustibles subjected the exposed steel to sufficiently high temperatures that it approached its own critical softening temperature. At the heart of the inferno, columns began buckling under the weight of the superjacent building and ceiling trusses could no longer support the weight of their overlying floors.

The first floor to break free of its weakened attachments to the inner and outer structural tubes triggered an irresistible cascade. The initial falling floor gathered up successively lower floors into a gravitationally accelerating and corporeally thickening stack. Simultaneously, the suddenly unsupported super-structure entered freefall and raced to catch the pancaking infrastructure, scarcely retarded in its descent by the resistance of cold steel below. Although the outer tube of steel columns was progressively dragged inward after the plummeting mass, it fortunately preserved its upper boundary of integrity just infinitesimally long enough to guide the bulk of the imploding debris to the footprint of the tower. Had the falling debris not been caged in this fashion, the devastation to the surrounding city blocks could have been far worse.

The kinetic energy released by the gravitational collapse of each tower was enough to pulverize the concrete and sheetrock in the crashing debris and to mobilize the particles into airborne debris surges with initial velocities of up to 60 miles per hour. At the same time, dust was shot into the air by outrushing jets from accordioning floors and by inrushing downdrafts entrained by the falling debris. The violent expulsion of air from the structure and substance of the buildings as they collapsed left—in place of two 1,360-foot-high towers—two 60-foot-high mounds of debris hidden under skyscraping clouds of smoke and dust. Enough heavy debris shouldered past the constraints of the outer tubes during the collapses of 1 and 2 WTC to rain down and destroy the rest of the World Trade Center, too: 3 and 7 WTC collapsed fully; 4, 5, and 6 WTC collapsed partly; and Tobin Plaza collapsed into the underground concourse, transforming it into a refuse pit 30 feet deep.

Despite their catastrophic endings, the Towers had remained standing long enough after impact to satisfy the buildings' formal safety parameters for evacuation. The North Tower stood for 1 hour 40 minutes after impact; the South Tower for 56 minutes. The Towers' stairwells had been expressly designed to permit full evacuation of each building in one hour. Yet it had been a matter of gravest concern after the 1993 bombing that only half the Towers' occupants had made it outside in the first hour. The last evacuees from the 1993 bombing needed four hours to clear the Towers. Subsequent critiques faulted the excessive narrowness of the stairwells, which had been pinched by the design premium on rentable floor space. Clearly, no such margin for dilatoriness was granted the victims of the 2001 attacks—or the hundreds of uniformed rescuers who perished in the collapses. Notwithstanding a majority of the Towers' occupants and those of the neighboring office buildings was able to evacuate, the toll of those who could not is horrendous past all imagining.

Even though the North Tower remained standing half-an-hour after the collapse of the South Tower and had been struck at a higher level than the South Tower, a significantly higher proportion of occupants of the North Tower—predominantly in the impact level and above—failed to escape. This paradox is explained by the quarter-hour grace that the occupants of the uppermost floors of the South Tower had, after witnessing the North Tower collision, to flee below the level of the later impact against the South Tower.

The Twin Towers were strong enough to stand long enough after impact to let a majority of the people in them escape. For this let us be profoundly thankful. For all those who were obliterated in the collisions, trapped in the conflagrations, or overtaken by the collapses—and the many thousands of their bereaved families and friends—let us weep. For a strength that will never collapse no matter how cruel the oppression, let us look to our own collective will and spirit—exemplified so poignantly by the heroic rescuers who died striving in the name of mercy.

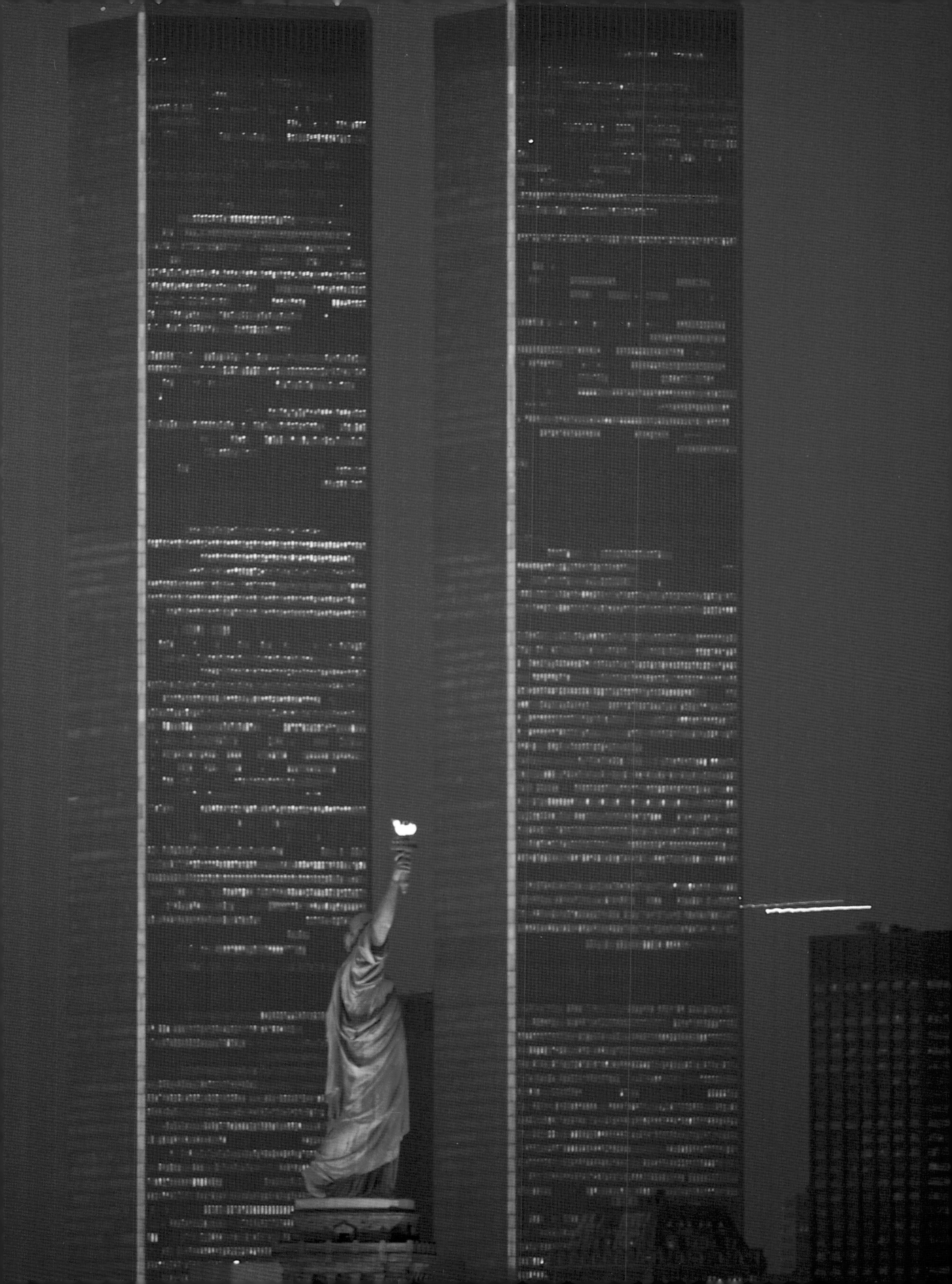

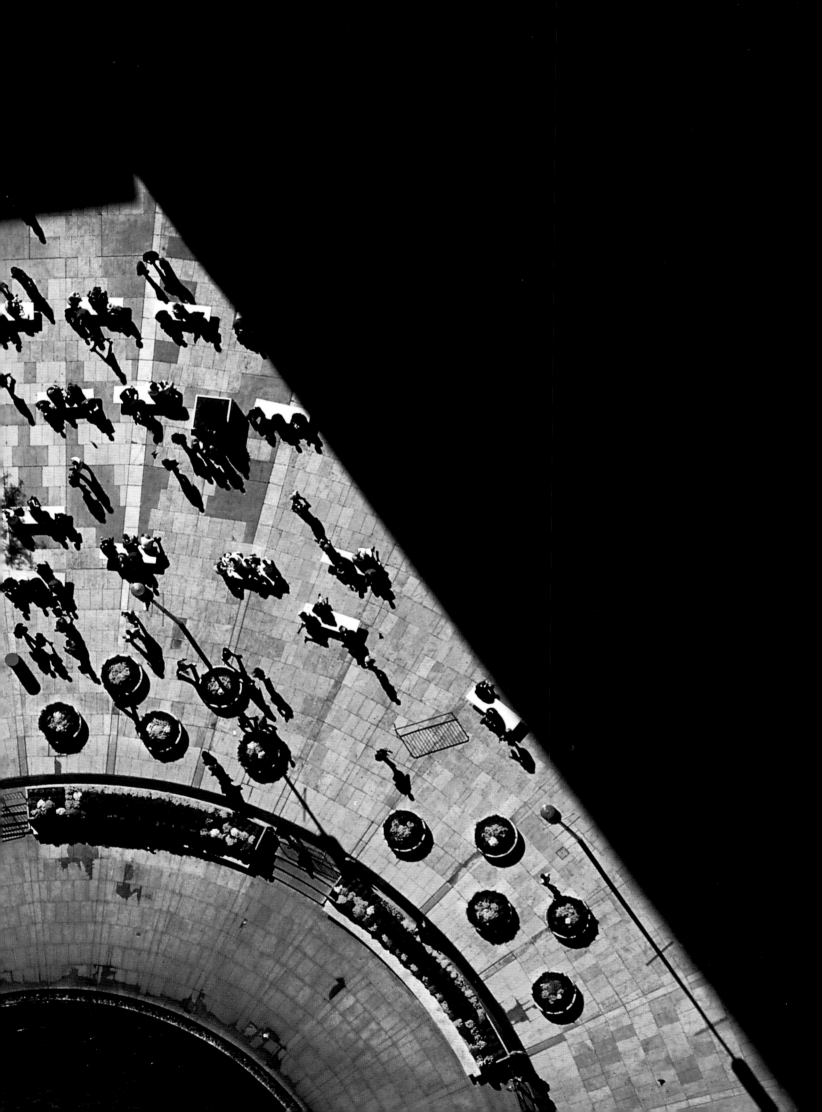